I0087451

ANTONYMS

Find the

OPPOSITES

Practice Questions

Jenny Pearson

COPYRIGHT

Antonyms: Find the Opposites Practice Questions

Jenny Pearson

Copyright © 2015 Kivett Publishing

All rights reserved, including the right to reproduce any portion of this book in any form.

Images licensed through Shutterstock.

Kivett Publishing

ISBN: 978-0-692-46606-3

Children's / educational / language arts

CONTENTS

INTRODUCTION

An **antonym** is a word that has the opposite meaning of another word.

Following are a few examples:

right / wrong

fun / boring

full / empty

PRACTICE QUESTIONS

Instructions: Circle a pair of antonyms in each of the following sentences.

Example 1: A (smile) is an upside down (frown).

Answer: smile / frown. A frown is the opposite of a smile.

Example 2: Every contest has a (loser) and a (winner).

Answer: winner / loser. A loser is the opposite of a winner.

(1) I thought I knew the right answer, but I was wrong.

(2) She laughed so hard that she cried.

(3) Do you know the answer to this question?

(4) When you remember what you forgot to do, sometimes it's too late.

(5) Dreams are nice, but nightmares wake me up screaming!

(6) I like sweet candy and sour grapes.

(7) Wouldn't it be fun if we could play all day and night?

(8) Don't try to enter through the exit.

(9) The party will start at two o'clock and end at four o'clock.

(10) He was very grumpy until the clown made him feel happy.

(11) Mom lost her house keys, but later found them in the car.

(12) I was the first kid at the carnival, and the last one to leave.

(13) She was sad until her friend came over and made her happy.

(14) I was afraid of the dark, but mom told me to be brave.

(15) His pants were too tight until he went on a diet, but then they were too loose.

(16) The suitcase was too heavy so he removed some items until it was light enough to carry.

(17) Prince Charming saved the beautiful princess from the dark ugly nightmare.

(18) The tide was too high to see the tide pools so we waited for the low tide.

(19) Dad was late because the traffic was stop and go.

(20) The kid was too short to ride the roller coaster, and too tall to go on the kiddie rides.

(21) The early show will be over before I get home from school, and the late show is for parents only.

(22) We can't play outdoors because it's raining, and if we stay indoors we have to be quiet.

(23) I'm young, and grandpa is old.

(24) I like my eggs hard boiled, while my dad likes his soft boiled.

(25) We reached the door just as the sign changed from open to closed.

(26) I thought her fake eyelashes were real.

(27) I wondered why my dad said it was neither here nor there.

(28) Tomorrow I will do what I should have done yesterday.

(29) Have you ever tried to push a door open when it says pull?

(30) Some roller coasters can go both forwards and backwards.

(31) Wanted: dead or alive.

(32) I live near the beach, but far from the mountains.

(33) The rubber ball will float, but the bowling ball will sink.

(34) The mouse looks tiny next to the huge elephant.

(35) Should the rich help the poor?

(36) It seems like my sister is always against whatever I am for.

(37) The gas gauge was broken so we thought that the gas tank was full when it was empty.

(38) The kind prince protected the princess from the cruel, fiery dragon.

(39) The magician can make the rabbit appear and disappear.

(40) My brother got wet, but I stayed dry because I used an umbrella.

(41) The boats go under the bridge while the cars go over the bridge.

(42) My brother ate all the candy so there was none left for me.

(43) I live on the left side of the school, and my friend lives on the right side.

(44) Mom likes the quiet, but I like to listen to loud music.

(45) For Halloween, I was an angel and my little brother was a devil.

(46) Please take the clean dishes out of the dishwasher before adding the dirty ones.

(47) It was so cold this morning that I needed a jacket, but by noon it was too hot for the jacket.

(48) My friend and I like the same ice-cream flavor, but like different types of cones.

(49) We raise the flag in the morning and lower it before it gets dark.

(50) It's fun playing follow the leader.

(51) I wasn't happy because my friend was sad.

(52) My favorite baseball pitcher started in the minor league, but was quickly drafted to a major league team.

(53) The race started at the park and ended at school.

(54) A giraffe has a long neck, and a bear has a short neck.

(55) It took all day and all night long to get to grandma's house.

(56) I can throw a slow pitch, but not a fast one.

(57) My sister can't swim so she has to stay in the shallow end of the pool and watch me dive into the deep end.

(58) My grandparents moved to a nearby town, but it's still too far for me to walk there.

(59) I thought he was going to deny that he did it, but he did admit to it!

(60) The ride looked dangerous, but it really was safe.

(61) We're supposed to whisper in the library, but I heard a kid yell to his friend.

(62) I want to sell my bike so I can buy a skateboard.

(63) I dislike asparagus, but really like ice-cream.

(64) The book got my attention from the very beginning, but I was disappointed with the ending.

(65) Dad painted the interior of our house, but hired someone to paint the exterior.

(66) The pasta tasted too bland until mom added herbs to make it spicy.

(67) My brother always turns the light on, but forgets to turn it off when he leaves the room.

(68) The teachers surprised the students with an ice-cream social.

(69) My friend is so polite that I can't believe her sister can be so rude.

(70) Dad had a lot of stress at work so he needs to relax this weekend.

(71) The king is wise, but the court jester is foolish.

(72) I thought I had all the correct answers, but one was wrong.

(73) I try to always agree with mom, but occasionally I have to disagree.

(74) My sister leaves a light on because she is afraid of the dark.

(75) We took the escalator up, and rode the elevator down.

(76) The adults were supposed to sit, but some had to stand because there weren't enough chairs.

(77) We got to the bus stop early, but the bus driver was late.

(78) They said it was a love-hate relationship.

(79) They grouped the dogs from the smallest to the largest.

(80) I sit in the front so I can see the chalkboard, but I miss my friend who sits in the back.

(81) Most of the textbooks are new, but a few are old.

(82) The boys let the girls go first.

(83) Did the teacher ask you or me to help with the clean-up?

(84) We thought we were supposed to go north, but the map showed that we should go south.

(85) My brother never gets to bed on time, but I always do.

(86) The parents watch their children play at the park.

(87) I thought it would be impossible to finish my chores, but it became possible when my friend helped me.

(88) I couldn't tell the difference between the real roses and the fake ones.

(89) Skateboarding is allowed at the park, but some people want it to be banned.

(90) I hope I just have friends, and no enemies.

(91) I was afraid I might break my expensive watch so I wore my cheap one.

(92) Grandpa talks about the past, but I want to talk about the future.

(93) Our house has an attic and basement.

(94) Dad sanded the rough wood so now it's smooth.

(95) We could see the valley from the top of the hill.

(96) My plane is scheduled to depart Los Angeles airport at 2:00 p.m. and arrive in Dallas at 6:45 p.m.

(97) I included all of my friends, except for one whom I accidently excluded from the invitation list.

(98) I was sound asleep when my talking alarm clock woke me up saying, "It's time for you to be awake."

(99) We left home at dawn, but didn't get back until dusk.

(100) I can do a forward flip, but I can't do a backward somersault.

CREATIVE EXERCISES

Write a sentence that uses the antonyms.

(1) son / daughter

_____

_____

_____

(2) fun / boring

_____

_____

_____

(3) top / bottom

_____

_____

_____

(4) inside / outside

_____

_____

_____

(5) soft / hard

_____

_____

_____

_____

(6) quick / slow

_____

_____

_____

_____

(7) wide / narrow

_____

_____

_____

_____

(8) yummy / yucky

_____

_____

_____

_____

(9) over / under

_____

_____

_____

_____

(10) black / white

_____

_____

_____

_____

(11) fair / unfair

_____

_____

_____

_____

(12) tight / loose

_____

_____

_____

_____

(13) hungry / full

_____

_____

_____

_____

(14) smallest / largest

_____

_____

_____

_____

(15) funny / serious

_____

_____

_____

_____

(16) alone / together

_____

_____

_____

_____

(17) above / below

_____

_____

_____

_____

(18) hello / goodbye

_____

_____

_____

_____

(19) recent / ancient

_____

_____

_____

_____

(20) husband / wife

_____

_____

_____

_____

ANSWER KEY

(1) right / wrong

(2) laughed / cried

(3) answer / question

(4) remember / forgot

(5) dreams / nightmares

(6) sweet / sour

(7) day / night

(8) enter / exit

(9) start / end

(10) grumpy / happy

(11) lost / found

(12) first / last

(13) sad / happy

(14) afraid / brave

(15) tight / loose

(16) heavy / light

(17) beautiful / ugly

(18) high / low

(19) stop / go

(20) short / tall

(21) early / late

(22) outdoors / indoors

(23) young / old

(24) hard / soft

(25) open / closed

(26) fake / real

(27) here / there

(28) tomorrow / yesterday

(29) push / pull

(30) forwards / backwards

(31) dead / alive

(32) near / far

(33) float / sink

(34) tiny / huge

(35) rich / poor

(36) against / for

(37) full / empty

(38) kind / cruel

(39) appear / disappear

(40) wet / dry

(41) under / over

(42) all / none

(43) left / right

(44) quiet / loud

(45) angel / devil

(46) clean / dirty

(47) cold / hot

(48) same / different

(49) raise / lower

(50) follow / leader

(51) happy / sad

(52) minor / major

(53) started / ended

(54) long / short

(55) day / night

(56) slow / fast

(57) shallow / deep

(58) nearby / far

(59) deny / admit

(60) dangerous / safe

(61) whisper / yell

(62) sell / buy

(63) dislike / like

(64) beginning / ending

(65) interior / exterior

(66) bland / spicy

(67) on / off

(68) teachers / students

(69) polite / rude

(70) stress / relax

(71) wise / foolish

(72) correct / wrong

(73) agree / disagree

(74) light / dark

(75) up / down

(76) sit / stand

(77) early / late

(78) love / hate

(79) smallest / largest

(80) front / back

(81) new / old

(82) boys / girls

(83) you / me

(84) north / south

(85) never / always

(86) parents / children

(87) impossible / possible

(88) real / fake

(89) allowed / banned

(90) friends / enemies

(91) expensive / cheap

(92) past / future

(93) attic / basement

(94) rough / smooth

(95) valley / hill

(96) depart / arrive

(97) included / excluded

(98) asleep / awake

(99) dawn / dusk

(100) forward / backward

www.ingramcontent.com/pod-product-compliance
Lightning Source LLC
Chambersburg PA
CBHW081154040426

42445CB00015B/1876